Credits:

Cheese
Photographs: VVV Gouda

Rotterdam
Photograph © Image Bank Rotterdam

The Hague
Photographs: Image Bank The Hague

The Efteling
Photographs: The Efteling and Christina Croad

Vermeer en Rembrandt
Vermeer - *Girl with a Pearl Earring*, The Mauritshuis, The Hague.
Rembrandt - *Self-portrait*, *View of Amsterdam from the Northwest*, Rijksmuseum, Amsterdam.

miffy®
Illustrations: Dick Bruna © copyright Mercis bv, 1953-2016

Van Gogh
Vincent van Gogh – *The Bedroom, Self-portrait as a Painter, Self-Portrait with Grey Felt Hat, Almond Blossom*, Van Gogh Museum, Amsterdam (Vincent van Gogh Foundation)

Anne Frank
Photograph: Anne Frank Foundation

First published in Belgium and Holland by Clavis Uitgeverij, Hasselt – Amsterdam, 2016
Copyright © 2016, Clavis Uitgeverij

English translation from the Dutch by Clavis Publishing Inc. New York
Copyright © 2016 for the English language edition: Clavis Publishing Inc. New York

Visit us on the web at www.clavisbooks.com

This Is the Netherlands written and illustrated by Mack
Original title: *Dit is Nederland*
Translated from the Dutch by Clavis Publishing

ISBN 978-1-60537-307-2 (US)
ISBN 978 90 448 2771 2 (European)

This book was printed in February 2016 at Publikum d.o.o., Slavka Rodica 6, Belgrade, Serbia

First Edition
10 9 8 7 6 5 4 3 2 1

THIS IS THE
Netherlands

Mack

Clavis

NEW YORK

THINGS THAT
THE NETHERLANDS
IS FAMOUS FOR

TULIPS

50 tulpen
€ 7.50

50 tulpen
€ 7.50

Dutch flowers are famous all over the world. Nowhere else will you find such colorful bouquets of roses, chrysanthemums and of course: tulips! The tulip came to the Netherlands from Turkey, and used to be very expensive. Three hundred years ago, a rare black tulip cost more than a large house! Nowadays you can buy a bunch of tulips with your pocket money.

Tulips often grow in groups of the same color,
but sometimes you see different colors all mixed together.

Which tulip used to be very rare?

TULIP FIELDS

The fields in the Netherlands are prettiest in the spring. That's when the tulips appear. The flowers shoot up from the ground, one color after another. Not just hundreds, but thousands! All the colors grow neatly in rows, dividing the Dutch landscape into blocks of pink, red, yellow, orange, purple and white tulips. Tourists from all over the world come to the Netherlands to see the tulip fields. Aren't they beautiful?

Which tulips aren't growing neatly in a straight line?

WINDMILLS

Windmills are found in many countries, but nowhere else are there as many as in the Netherlands. Almost every city has its own windmill. In the past there were even more. Windmills are very strong. They catch the wind with their large sails. The wind turns the sails and powers the millstone, which grinds everything very fine. That's how a mill grinds rough grain into fine flour, which is used to make bread. Mmmmm!

Windmills wait for the wind to blow.
A stiff wind will turn the sails around
and around.

Which windmill isn't getting much wind?

When it starts to freeze, everyone in the Netherlands gets excited. Is there ice on the canals? Is it thick enough? Can we go skating yet? On a beautiful, cold winter's day, you'll see lots of people out on the frozen ponds. One is learning to skate, leaning on a chair, while another does pretty figures on the ice, and yet others are dressed warmly for a long skating trip. The Dutch look forward to it all year long!

Which girls are still learning to skate?

SPEED SKATING

Do you know what a Dutch person likes even better than skating?
Speed skating! Speed skating is done wearing sharp skates and a fitted
suit. The curves are the hardest. The skaters must cross their legs while
going full speed. That can sometimes lead to serious crashes, but those
who are good at it really fly over the ice! The Dutch are good skaters and
almost always win a bronze, a silver or even a gold medal at the Winter
Olympic Games.

Skating marathons are held on long rivers. The most famous one is the Elfstedentocht in Friesland. It starts early in the morning and ends after dark. If you finish after the course is closed, you don't get a medal!

Which skater is going the wrong way?

CHEESE

Dutch cheeses are often made in the shape of a big, round wheel. But cheese is sold by the slice in the shops. In the past, every Dutch village had its own kind of cheese: some with holes, others with spices or seeds. Every city had a cheese market where cheese was weighed, graded and sold. A few markets still exist. Do you want to see one? Then visit Alkmaar, Edam or Gouda in the summertime.

A round Gouda cheese weighs 26 pounds. You can't even lift it!

Which is the piece of cumin cheese (with seeds)?

COWS

The cow you see the most in the Netherlands is white with black spots. This breed is called Holstein Friesian and doesn't get fat, but produces a lot of delicious milk. That's why it's so popular. You see this cow in other countries too. Just like the Dutch people, black-and-white cows are very curious. They always watch as you walk past.

Cows love grass and clover, and flowers too.
Just like butterflies!

Can you spot the Dutch Belted? This cow has a sort of belt around his waist.

CLOGS

Clogs are shoes made out of wood. In the past, almost everyone walked around the Dutch countryside in clogs. They were carved from tree trunks and then sanded and painted. It's not easy to walk in clogs. You have to squeeze your toes with every step. Dancing in clogs is even harder. Even so, there's a dance that you can only dance in clogs. Can you guess what it's called? That's right! The clog dance!

The clog dance.

Which shoe is a clog?

THE SEA, BEACHES AND DUNES

THE NORTH SEA

The Netherlands lies on the North Sea. From the beach, the sea looks like a giant lake. You can't even see the other side. And yet the North Sea is quite small for a sea, and very shallow. If the tallest church tower in the Netherlands stood on the bottom of the sea, you would see its spire sticking up out of the water. Many animals live in the North Sea: crabs, shrimp and fish… even a few species of shark!

There's another sea in between the West Frisian Islands: the Wadden Sea. These sandbars are a favorite spot of sea lions!

Do you recognize the seagulls?

There are endless beaches on the shores of the North Sea. The beaches are made of soft sand—wonderful for lying on and enjoying the sun. Or you can play on the beach and perhaps build a nice sand castle, or dig a deep hole that you can hide in. This fancy building is called the Kurhaus and is located on the boulevard in Scheveningen. Tourists come to Scheveningen to walk and sunbathe on the wide beaches.

You can play on the beach,
or you can quietly listen to the waves.

Who is a little sunburned?

THE DUNES

The Dutch coast is lined with grassy hills. Sand dunes! The dunes are so tall that the sea can't get past them. They make sure that the Netherlands isn't flooded by the North Sea. Many animals live in the dunes. Mostly rabbits, which make their holes in the dunes. You also see many deer and foxes. The largest residents are the Highland cattle. Every day they come and drink from a dune pool.

How many rabbits do you see in the dunes?

Which animals are hiding in the dunes?

LAND FROM WATER

A long time ago most of the Netherlands wasn't even land. It was water! Large areas of water. Because the Netherlands is so small, clever engineers figured out how to drain the lakes and turn them into dry land. They used windmills to pump the water out of the lakes. That's how new areas of land, the polders, were created, where many houses now stand and cows now graze. Thank you, windmills!

Windmills pumped the Dutch lakes dry
and made new areas of land, called polders.

Which houses are lower than sea level?

TASTY TREATS

POFFERTJES

Poffertjes are a typical Dutch specialty. They look like small, puffy pancakes. A good poffertjes cook can make a lot of them at once. He uses a big pan with lots of little holes. Each hole is filled with batter. The cook turns the poffertjes really fast with a fork. When both sides are brown, he puts them on a plate. A little butter, a little powdered sugar, and they're ready to eat!

Powdered sugar goes well
with a plate of poffertjes.

Typically Dutch:
a cookie with tea.

Do these Dutch sweets look familiar?

STAMPPOT

The Dutch love stamppot. To make stamppot, you mash potatoes and vegetables together. Often a meatball or a sausage is eaten alongside. There's stamppot with kale, or with Belgian endive, or "hot lightning", with apples and bacon. Hutspot is made with carrots and onion. Do you know what stamppot with green beans and white beans is called?
Bare bottoms in the grass!

Typical Dutch dishes: hutspot, endive stamppot and split pea soup with rye bread and bacon.

Have you tried these favorite Dutch foods?

DROP

Drop is a candy that you find in every sweet shop in the Netherlands. It comes in all forms, colors and sizes. Some drop is sweet, some drop is a little salty. All kinds of drop are made from the same root: the licorice root. A piece is cut off and the rest goes back in the ground to continue growing. The root is ground, boiled and mixed with honey or sugar. If you let this mixture dry in a mold, you have drop. Yum!

There are many kinds of drop.
Farmer's drop, drop ropes,
drop buttons, drop sticks, honey drop,
drop kitties, drop coins, sweet drop,
salty drop, drop keys, drop lozenges
and more.

Which of these typical Dutch sweets look good to you?

HERRING

Herring is a fish that lives in the North Sea. In the winter, the herring is left alone, but in the summer, fishermen throw out their nets and haul in the herring catch. On the first day that the herring fishermen sail out, Dutch ports and villages are decorated with flags. That's why this holiday is called Flag Day. Finally the new herring is in! First it's cleaned, and then served with its tail still on. You grab it by the tail to eat it. Some people eat a whole herring in one bite!

A woman in costume presents the new herring—the first herring of the year. With onions!

What Dutch foods from the North Sea do you recognize?

BEAUTIFUL PLACES

AMSTERDAM

Amsterdam is the capital of the Netherlands. It is also the biggest city. You can identify Amsterdam right away from the beautiful houses alongside little canals. Each canal house is different. Many front doors sit above the street, you have to step up when you enter. That's because the canals used to flood quite often!

There's a nice view of the Anne Frank House, with the West Tower behind it, from the bridge on the Prinsengracht.

There are bikes everywhere in Amsterdam!

Which canal houses have step-gabled roofs?

AMSTERDAM

The canals of Amsterdam are as famous as the city itself. All year long, you can tour the city center by boat. Along the way you'll see houseboats—boats that people live in. On holidays, Amsterdam's canals are overflowing with many boats. Especially on King's Day, the king's birthday, when the boats are all filled with party-goers dressed in orange.

Amsterdam's Royal Palace was built to show the world how wealthy the Netherlands was back then.

Do you see the houseboat?

ROTTERDAM

You can tell Rotterdam is a modern city from its buildings. Rotterdam's apartments aren't boring and square, but pointy or crooked. Or built to look like a pencil sharpener! A few houses in Rotterdam are shaped like cubes with slanted sides. The Central Station (above) looks like it's folded, with little pyramids on top. Typical Rotterdam!

Rotterdam has houses shaped like cubes. All the walls are slanted!

Which houses are located in Rotterdam?

ROTTERDAM

Rotterdam has one of the largest ports in the world. The Nieuwe Maas river flows through the city towards the North Sea. Ships sail to and fro every day with their cargo. Old boats are moored in the smaller harbors, where you'll find restaurants and outdoor patios. In the background you see the red Willems Bridge, one of the many remarkable bridges in modern Rotterdam.

The Leuve Harbor of Rotterdam with the Euromast in the background.

Which boat is carrying the most containers?

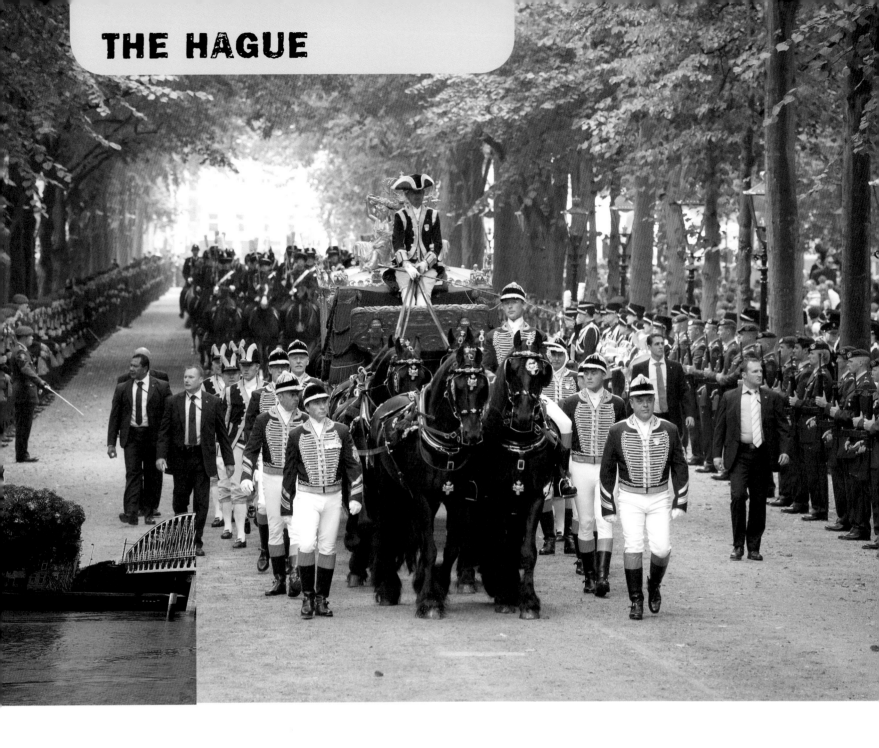

The king of the Netherlands lives in The Hague. On Princes' Day, the king and the queen ride out in their Golden Carriage. Led by uniformed footmen, the procession goes across town to the Knights' Hall. There, the ministers await the moment when the king gives the Royal Speech. He says what the government will do in the following year. This tradition takes place every year, on the third Tuesday in September.

*The king and queen's procession on Princes' Day
always starts at Noordeinde Palace,
the working palace of the king in The Hague.*

Who isn't a footman?

Panorama Mesdag in The Hague is one of the biggest paintings in the world. The painting goes all the way around in a circle, and you can stand in the middle. If you were to lay it out in a straight line, it would be longer than a football field. Panorama Mesdag shows Scheveningen, the beach resort of The Hague, as it looked long ago. The dunes and church towers are still there, but the fishing boats no longer lie on the beach, but in the harbor.

This girl is looking at a little Golden Carriage in front of the Knights' Hall.
The miniature carriage is part of tourist attraction Madurodam,
where a replica Netherlands is built in small scale.

Can you name the king's possessions?

UTRECHT

Utrecht is a city with wide canals where you can enjoy a nice boat ride. There are terraces, tall trees and houses all along the water. Utrecht is located in the middle of the Netherlands. It is the city with the highest tower in the country: the Dom. It's also the city of miffy. Artist Dick Bruna has his own museum in the old center of Utrecht, with original drawings of the popular bunny.

The Dom of Utrecht is the highest tower in the Netherlands.

Utrecht has a museum of music boxes and hurdy-gurdies.

Which of these three cities is Utrecht?

DELFT

Delft is one of the prettiest small cities in the world. The entire city center is like a museum. When you enter Delft, you cross a drawbridge and then pass through a gate. Delft is famous because Prince William of Orange lived here. He was the father of the Netherlands and was killed in the Prinsenhof in Delft. You can still see the bullet holes in the wall!

Many houses in Delft burned down because of a lightning strike in 1536.

The pretty blue color of this porcelain is called "Delft blue."
On which tile do you see children playing?

ZAANSE SCHANS

There are more than a dozen windmills in the Zaanse Schans. Most of the windmills look out over the water and each one has a name. The Cat grinds pigments, the Seeker mills oil from seeds, the Clover Leaf saws wood, and there's also a brick mill and a grain mill. The windmills used to be spread all over the region, but they're much prettier all together. That's why they were put on boats and taken to the Zaanse Schans. Nice, huh?

Tourists like to take pictures with the Zaanse Schans windmills.

The Cat Mill makes dyestuffs. Which colors have run together?

THE EFTELING

Photographs: The Efteling and Christina Croad

Fairy tales come to life in the Efteling, the Netherlands' most famous amusement park. Here in the fairy-tale wood, you'll meet Sleeping Beauty, Red Riding Hood, Cinderella, the Story Tree, Puss-in-Boots and Snow White. Do you see Hansel and Gretel next to the gingerbread house? The witch has taken Hansel prisoner and wants to fatten him up for dinner. Gretel must save him! But how?

The Efteling's fairy-tale wood was created by Dutch artist Anton Pieck. The figures, buildings and animals there are famous in the Netherlands.

Flying Pagoda.

Long-neck.

Gold-Donkey.

Which fairy tale characters do you recognize?

Muiderslot is one of the best-preserved castles in the Netherlands.
It was built long ago to protect its residents from their enemies. When
the drawbridge over the moat is up, no one can get in, not even the
strongest knights. Slot Loevestein is another beautiful castle. During the
Eighty Years' War, the nobleman Hugo Grotius was imprisoned there.
Luckily he escaped by hiding... in a chest of books!

The prettiest castle in the Netherlands:
De Haar Castle.

Can you name the knight's equipment?

Rembrandt van Rijn

Jeroen Bosch

Anne Frank

FAMOUS DUTCH PEOPLE

Hugo de Groot

Erasmus

Willem van Oranje

VERMEER AND REMBRANDT

Vermeer — Girl with a Pearl Earring, *The Mauritshuis, The Hague*

Rembrandt van Rijn and Johannes Vermeer are two of the most famous painters from the Netherlands. They lived hundreds of years ago during the Dutch Golden Age, when the Netherlands was bigger and richer than it is now. Vermeer painted the beautiful *Girl with a Pearl Earring*. He loved the colors blue and yellow. Rembrandt was perhaps the best painter in the world during his lifetime. His painting *The Night Watch*, in the Rijksmuseum in Amsterdam, attracts thousands of admirers every year.

Rembrandt – Self-portrait, *Rijksmuseum, Amsterdam.*

Rembrandt – View of Amsterdam from the Northwest, *Rijksmuseum, Amsterdam.*

This is how Rembrandt saw Amsterdam. How many windmills do you see?

miffy is the most famous bunny in the Netherlands and maybe in the whole world. Her books are read in many different countries. Children in Japan and China are crazy about miffy. The artist who created miffy is Dick Bruna. He wrote the first book about the beloved bunny for his own son, more than sixty years ago. And today miffy is world-famous!

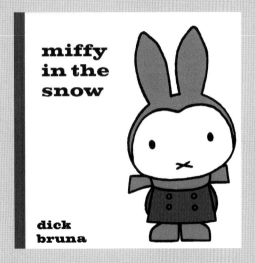

miffy's books are translated into many languages.

Which miffy is ready for the snow?

VAN GOGH

Vincent van Gogh — The Bedroom, Self-portrait as a Painter, Self-Portrait with Grey Felt Hat, Almond Blossom, *Van Gogh Museum, Amsterdam (Vincent van Gogh Foundation)*

He cut off a piece of his own ear, only sold one painting during his lifetime, and was often very depressed. Vincent van Gogh lived his life with passion, and you can see that in his paintings. He painted in a fury and wrote hundreds of letters about his artwork to his brother Theo. Theo kept all his brother's paintings and now you can see many of them in the Van Gogh Museum in Amsterdam.

Vincent van Gogh painted himself as no one else had: with lots of color, lots of emotion and lots of brush strokes.

Vincent van Gogh liked to paint sunflowers. Do you see them?

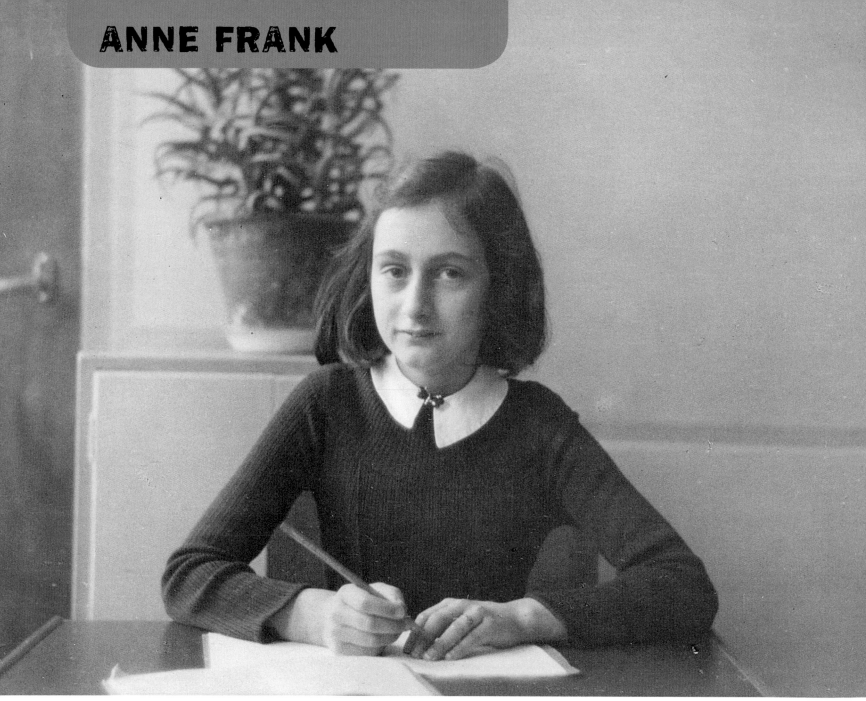

ANNE FRANK

Photograph: Anne Frank Foundation

During World War II, a girl named Anne Frank hid from the Germans. She lived with her parents and her sister in a secret room in a big house in Amsterdam, the Achterhuis. Anne Frank wrote in her diary every day. After Anne was discovered and died at a young age, her diary became world-famous. In her diary, Anne Frank describes her own life: the life of a young girl during wartime.

A heavy bookcase …

*… hid a secret stair
to Anne Frank's hiding place.*

Why did Anne Frank become famous?